CHAVISMO WITHOUT CHÁVEZ

Anticipated Challenges for Regional and U.S. National Security

The Menges Hemispheric Security Project of
the Center for Security Policy

Presents the Proceedings of:

The Third Annual Capitol Hill National Security
Briefing on Latin America

Thursday, May 9, 2013

Washington, D. C.

©2014 Center for Security Policy Press
Washington, D.C.

1

CHAVISMO WITHOUT CHÁVEZ

Anticipated Challenges for Regional and U.S. National Security

Michael Braun -Congressman Jeff Duncan - Douglas Farah

Dr. Luis Fleischman - Frank J. Gaffney, Jr. - Nancy Menges

Roger Noriega - Jon Perdue - Martin Rodil - Congressman Matt Salmon

Frank J. Gaffney, Jr.
Publisher

Adam Savit
Editor

ISBN 978-0-9850292-2-7

PRINTED IN THE UNITED STATES OF AMERICA

1 2 3 4 5 6 7 8 9 10

Second Edition

THE CENTER FOR SECURITY POLICY
1901 Pennsylvania Avenue, Suite 201 Washington, DC 20006
Phone: (202) 835-9077 | Email: info@securefreedom.org
For more information, please see securefreedom.org

Book design by Adam Savit
Cover design by David Reaboi

Contents

Introductory Remarks

REPRESENTATIVE JEFF DUNCAN, 3rd DISTRICT OF SOUTH CAROLINA

Chairman, Subcommittee on Oversight and Management Efficiency, House Committee on Homeland Security

REPRESENTATIVE MATT SALMON, 5TH DISTRICT OF ARIZONA

Chairman, Subcommittee on Western Hemisphere, House Committee on Foreign Affairs (Adapted for publication)

R EP. DUNCAN: I'm going to begin by thanking the Center for Security Policy for hosting this excellent and timely panel discussion today. My office, specifically Rebecca Ulrich, has worked with all these panelists, and I readily admit that their depth of understanding has helped me develop a clearer and deeper view of the challenges and opportunities that exist in Latin America today.

The U.S. possesses longstanding relations with our neighbors. Simple geography and shared economic, political, cultural, and security interests fuel these relationships. Yet, I believe the U.S. must do a better job of engaging our allies and partners here in the region. I want to commend Chairman Salmon for recently taking a CODEL [congressional delegation] to this region to start understanding some of the relationships that we need, and also to continue talking about the Iranian threat here in the Western Hemisphere. Our security and interests depend on relationships that we have here in this hemisphere.

We face a myriad of challenges in Latin America. Exploding criminal violence from transnational groups, growing sophistication from drug trafficking organizations or DTOs, and illicit activities in smuggling contraband and people threaten every country in the region in one form or another. Honduras, for example, is the deadliest place in the world, with more people per capita murdered than any other country, including Iraq and Afghanistan. Mexico, which shares over two thousand miles of border with the U.S., has seen over sixty thousand of its citizens brutally murdered by DTOs and other criminal groups. This violence has spilled over into this country, into U.S. border towns, and we've seen Mexican DTOs operating in other U.S. cities.

In March, SOUTHCOM [Southern Command] Commander General John Kelly testified before the Senate Armed Services Committee, and he highlighted several key regional challenges: a crime and terror nexus between DTOs and terrorist organizations; Iran's increasing activity in the Western Hemisphere; a growth in outreach by external extremist groups from the Middle East and Africa and South Asia within the Western Hemisphere; and the expanding role of China in the region. I'll stop right there and mention I was in Texas at the King Ranch talking to their security forces with responsibility for securing their 830,000 acres. They catch folks coming across their property that are OTMs, Other Than Mexicans. They're catching African, Middle Eastern, and Asian folks in just east of or north of Brownsville and eastern Corpus Christi in Texas. I thought that was an interesting statistic, and it just continues to fuel my alarm. With this in view, I was encouraged to hear General Kelly's frank assessment following the legislation I introduced last Congress to address some of these issues.

The Countering Iran in the Western Hemisphere Act was passed by Congress and signed by the President into Public Law 112-220 last December. The Center for Security Policy was instrumental in supporting this legislation and helping raise awareness not only in Congress but also nationwide. I certainly appreciate your efforts. This law states that the policy of the U.S. is to use a comprehensive government-wide strategy to counter Iran's growing hostile presence and activity in the Western Hemisphere by working together with U.S. allies and partners in the region to mutually deter the threats by Iran, the Iranian Revolutionary Guard, the Qods Force, and Hezbollah. The law requires the State Department to deliver a report to Congress with an assessment of the threat and a strategy to meet that threat. Earlier this week on Monday, I met with the Assistant Secretary of State for the Bureau of Western Hemisphere Affairs, Roberta Jacobson, on this issue. I understand the State Department is on track to submit this report on time next month. With last month's bombing attack in Boston and the foiled operation in Canada the next day reportedly backed by al-Qaeda elements in Iran, I believe that this report will be an essential tool to counter the threat that Iran poses to the U.S. and our friends in this hemisphere.

I'll also mention that Chairman McCaul, Chairman of the House Homeland Security Committee, was on the subcommittee last year that I now chair, and he led on a CODEL to South America to visit with officials in Mexico, Colombia, Paraguay, and Argentina to focus on Hezbollah, the Tri-border region, and Iran's activity there. Chairman McCaul understands these issues well, and I think it's important to note our shared vision, which I think will benefit us going forward.

Compounding these challenges from Iran is Venezuela. With the death of Hugo Chávez two months ago, I had hoped for a new opportunity and fresh start for the people of Venezuela to freely and fairly choose a leader who would pursue justice and good governance domestically and pursue peace with its neighbors. I don't know that we're going to get that. Venezuela is off to a rocky start with unclear and potentially fraudulent election results. The election of Nicolás Maduro, and Maduro's continuance of Chávez's flaming rhetoric and antipathy towards the U.S. provide many reasons for concern that I'm sure this symposium will examine closely.

While I could dwell more on these challenges, I want to use my remaining time to mention some of the exciting opportunities that we have today in the Western Hemisphere. First, we have excellent law enforcement and military cooperation within the region and growing intelligence sharing with many of our neighbors. For instance, last year, the South Carolina National Guard formed a partnership with Colombia as the newest partnership under the U.S. military's State Partnership Program to help train the Colombian military in democratic principles and healthy civilian-military relations. In addition, the Colombians have visited South Carolina to view operations that we have occurring. So I look forward to that type of growing relationship among other Latin American friends and partners. The U.S. Department of Homeland Security also has a Federal Law Enforcement Training Facility located in El Salvador that's been instrumental in building partner capacity to disrupt the efforts of transnational criminal organizations.

Second, trade opportunities abound. The Latin American and the Caribbean region as a whole is one of the fastest growing regional trading partners for the U.S. with the U.S. maintaining six free trade agreements with eleven countries in the region. With three Latin American countries participating in the TPP, or Trans-Pacific Partnership negotiations— Mexico, Chile, and Peru, as well as Canada—I'm very interested to see how this agreement will impact the Western Hemisphere. Additionally, DHS and the State Department have been in discussions with the governments in Chile, Brazil, and Uruguay about the criteria for joining the visa waiver program. I look forward to seeing how these conversations proceed.

Finally, we have a tremendous energy opportunity here in the Western Hemisphere, home to nearly a third of the world's oil, and we're finding more and more every day. Latin America and the Caribbean region have nearly three hundred and thirty-seven billion barrels of oil, over twenty percent of the crude reserves. The U.S. also possesses vast reserves of oil, natural gas, and shale gas reserves. This abundance of resources within the U.S. has opened up new possibilities for the U.S. to export, specifically LNG, Liquefied Natural Gas, in significant quantities.

And I know the Caribbean nations are very, very interested in receiving that LNG to help fuel their energy needs. However, the U.S. Department of Energy has put up roadblocks delaying the export licenses and also the licenses for the building out of the export terminals, calling for new review and a questioning period. These are just delay tactics that put off implementation of things like the Keystone Pipeline. This has resulted in poor U.S. leadership and has allowed other countries to fill the void. Venezuela has been able to exert considerable influence in the region through its Petrocaribe program, which has allowed it to provide oil to eighteen Central American and Caribbean nations on preferential terms since 2005. With Chávez's death, the future of the Petrocaribe program is unclear. I think there's an opportunity for the U.S. to step into that.

I believe the U.S. should show leadership on energy policy to our allies and our partners in the Western Hemisphere. The most fundamental action we can take is to implement the U.S.-Mexican Transboundary Hydrocarbon Reservoirs Agreement, which was signed by the U.S. and Mexico in 2012. I believe this agreement will provide more certainty to the energy market, lower energy costs, and create American jobs by safely opening up more areas in the Gulf of Mexico for exploration and production and will move us closer to working with Mexico to get those resources that are basically owned by both countries. I, along with Chairman Matt Salmon and Chairman Doc Hastings introduced H.R. 1613 to approve and implement the terms of this agreement, and we look forward to seeing this legislation move quickly through the Natural Resources Committee.

In conclusion, while the Western Hemisphere faces some serious challenges, I believe we also have some great opportunities. The bottom line is that the U.S. needs to lead. We've got to show some leadership, we need to engage our allies and partners in the region to a greater extent than we have in the past, I would say. Latin America has increasingly become independent from the U.S., and I'm encouraged by the economic growth that I've seen by a lot of the countries. For example, the zero unemployment in Panama and very low unemployment in Colombia provide many opportunities for growth. However the influence of Venezuelan-led Bolivian Alliance of the Americas, or ALBA, has contributed to the anti-American sentiment in the region, and the election of Nicolás Maduro may only foment more of these views. With many challenges facing our hemisphere, the U.S. must engage more frequently with our neighbors to come to common definitions of the threats we face, which are real, and to develop strategies to successfully defend our interests. Thank you everyone for helping our office as we move forward in trying to make America more secure in countering these real threats to our national security. I certainly appreciate it. God bless you all.

REP. SALMON: In keeping with my commitment to democratic values and the rule of law, as Chairman of the House Subcommittee on the Western Hemisphere I plan to continue monitoring the dire situation in Venezuela. I am increasingly concerned about the future of Venezuela as the Nicolás Maduro administration has been employing the same authoritarian practices of the Chávez regime by limiting the participation of the opposition, intervening in the development of the economy, and threatening the region's commitment to democratic values.

The results of the April 14th elections are still highly questionable. In my opinion, the outcome has the potential to destabilize Venezuela. Reports of irregularities at polling stations and acts of violence perpetrated by Chavista supporters against members of the opposition serve to demonstrate that Nicolás Maduro and his Chavista camp will use the same despotic tactics to hold on to power as his predecessor. I believe action is needed. That is why members of the Subcommittee and I have urged Secretary of State John Kerry and the Obama administration to call for an official audit of the election.

With that said, if Nicolás Maduro remains in power he will continue to squander Venezuelan resources to further the work of his mentor, the late Hugo Chávez. Chávez mismanaged Venezuela's abundant natural resources, including the vast oil wealth, by supporting undemocratic regimes and other bad actors around the world. Today, with diminishing oil production, Venezuela is a clear example of the consequences of leftist and populist policies. While I do not expect much to change if Nicolás Maduro manages to stay in power, I do not think that he will be able to maintain the same level of financial assistance to Cuba, the ALBA countries or the Petrocaribe oil program. I am sure that officials in Havana and Managua are seriously concerned that the Venezuelan cash cow is about to run dry. We must pay close attention to any developments or shifts in this area.

Moreover, having inherited an under-performing economy plagued by inflation and scarcity, Nicolás Maduro will surely face increasing levels of violence and opposition to his policies making it difficult for him to hold on to power. Because of this and his undemocratic reputation, Maduro and Chávez loyalists in the Venezuelan National Assembly can be expected to use all means possible to continue their unsustainable leftist policies to the detriment of the Venezuelan people.

The world can expect to see the deterioration of the Venezuelan economy, democratic principles, and an increased use of cowardly intimidation tactics against those individuals who dare to speak out against Chavismo and the revolution. Because of this, my Subcommittee intends to shed light on these and similar undemocratic power grabs that threaten to deteriorate democratic institutions and values throughout the Western Hemisphere.

PANEL ONE

LUIS FLEISCHMAN, PH.D., SENIOR ADVISER TO THE MENGES HEMISPHERIC SECURITY PROJECT, ADJUNCT PROFESSOR AT THE FAU WILKES HONORS COLLEGE AND AUTHOR OF *LATIN AMERICA IN THE POST-CHÁVEZ ERA*

> Topic: The likely composition of the post-Chávez Venezuelan Regime, how Chavismo operates on a regional level, and how Brazil and Argentina have responded

JON PERDUE, DIRECTOR OF LATIN AMERICAN PROGRAMS AT THE FUND FOR AMERICAN STUDIES AND AUTHOR OF *WAR OF ALL THE PEOPLE: THE NEXUS OF LATIN AMERICAN RADICALISM AND MIDDLE EASTERN TERORRISM*

> Topic: Asymmetric Warfare as carried out by the Bolivarian Revolution, and its implications for regional and U.S. national security

MARTIN RODIL, SENIOR POLICY ANALYST, VISION AMERICAS

> Topic: Iranian Activities inside Venezuela and the ALBA Countries

MODERATOR: FRANK J. GAFFNEY, JR., PRESIDENT AND CEO, THE CENTER FOR SECURITY POLICY

L UIS FLEISCHMAN: I want to thank Nancy Menges for putting together this conference. I also want to express my gratitude to Frank Gaffney, Christine Brim, Ben Lerner, Adam Savit and the entire staff of the Center for Security Policy. Likewise, I also want to thank Congressmen Matt Salmon and Jeff Duncan for their leadership on this issue and particularly Congressman Duncan on his wonderful piece of legislation, "Countering the Iranian presence in the Western Hemisphere." What I'm going to discuss now is how I view Venezuela at this time. I'm going to discuss the regional context in which events in Venezuela are taking place. Finally, I will discuss some policy prescriptions—particularly diplomatic policy prescriptions.

As you all know, what is happening now in Venezuela is that Nicolás Maduro won the recent presidential election. Maduro was Chávez's vice president and right-hand man, and is now the leader of the PSUV [Partido Socialista Unido de Venezuela], the political party founded by Chávez. At present there is a recount because Maduro only won the election by a small margin. However, the Electoral Commission decided that they are only going to count about twelve thousand boxes, which is about forty-six per cent of the vote.

What is interesting is that the Commission approved the election of Maduro on the one hand, but on the other are going ahead with a recount. Now what is the problem? The problem is that if the recount eventually is decided in favor of Capriles, the opposition candidate, how can they remove one president and put another is not clear to me. But what is clear is that the Venezuelan Electoral Commission is absolutely subjugated to the will of the Chavistas. Therefore, Maduro is likely to stay in power.

Nonetheless, there are certain things that are happening here. Even if we accept the results announced by the national Electoral Commission, the fact is that virtually a month after Chávez's death his successor received far fewer votes than Chávez received in October (Chávez won by a nine percent or ten percent margin, and Maduro won only by two percent). This is three or four months after Chávez actually swept the municipal and the governorship elections in Venezuela. Basically, twenty out of twenty three states are in the hands of Hugo Chávez's party, whereas only three states are in the hands of the opposition. So all of a sudden, the April 14th elections take place, and even if we accept the result, we are seeing a far narrower margin that Maduro actually won by. Now, what happened here? In my view, two things happened. On the one hand, Maduro lacks charisma; the charisma is not there. Hugo Chávez had a tremendous ability to provide a living promise. That means that despite the fact that the economy was in very bad shape and despite the fact that there was a big debt and food shortages and inflation and so on and so forth, still the personality of Chávez was able to provide justifications and attract people and be popular among the poor people. However, once this charisma disappears, Maduro will have to deliver the goods. That means he'll have to work hard to make sure that the economy goes in the right direction and that the people's needs are properly satisfied. This is unlikely to happen.

There is a second element that was lost in this election and that's the element of intimidation. Hugo Chávez's personality was able to intimidate the opposition. And if you compare the way in which Capriles ran his campaign for the October election, and the way he ran it now for the April election, you see now a Capriles that is by far more courageous. And not only that he's more courageous and confronts Maduro, he also seems not to even have much respect for Maduro. With Chávez, Capriles behaved like a pussycat. All of a sudden, this is changing. For the first time the opposition denounced electoral fraud. The opposition also demanded a recount. That would not have happened under Chávez. So two elements have been lost here, the charismatic element and the element of intimidation. And this is going to generate a reaction on the part of Venezuelans. We are going to see Venezuelans organizing more and more against the government. Now, what would be the natural reaction of the government? I don't expect Maduro to react by being open to the opposition and inviting the opposition to negotiate. In fact, Maduro is going to react with violence. And I think the violent scenes that we saw last week in the Assembly where members of the opposition were hit by the Chavistas while the president of the Assembly sat laughing, is a clear indication of the way the government is going to react.

I don't see Maduro responding by calling for a dialogue or inclusion. Therefore, we are going to see the repressive apparatus increasing and probably elections will be eventually eliminated altogether, as only Chávez could sustain the element of elections. I don't think Maduro can sustain it. Therefore, I think the Venezuelan regime is going to be a more repressive regime. And if the regime becomes repressive, it will have all the advantages. And the advantage that they have is what the Chávez regime has been building in the last fourteen years. It has co-opted the military by purging eight hundred officers in the Venezuelan military. So that means that those who expect that the military will stand with the people is an illusion. Don't expect that. I don't think this is going to happen. In addition, Chávez created his own paramilitary force. And finally, the regime controls the main natural resources and sources of employment. The government can fire and hire people as well; buy people and bribe people as much as it wants. There might be a situation here where the authoritarian rule of Chavismo may well perpetuate itself forever, and that is not a good situation.

Now there is a second element by which I think the Maduro government can get more support and that is in the international context. For example, what happened a day after Maduro was recognized as the new elected president of Venezuela, the Union of South American Nations (UNASUR)—a South American organization established to promote regional integration—convened in Lima within twenty-four hours after the election and declared Maduro the winner of the election. They decided to recognize Maduro as the winner and at the same time they supported a recount. In other words, South American countries became accomplices of the Venezuelan Electoral Commission and the Chávez regime altogether.

Now, what is happening in the regional context is crucial to understand the survival of the Maduro regime. I would say that the main country responsible for the support of Hugo Chávez is none other than Brazil.

In the region there are countries such as those that belong to ALBA (the Bolivarian Alliance), namely those countries that are associated with Chávez such as Nicaragua, Ecuador, Bolivia and Cuba. But there are also countries that are more moderate or social democracies such as Brazil, Uruguay, and a few others. The latter have also supported the government of Venezuela, because they view the left as a movement and this particular moment as the time of the left. They don't want to separate between the extreme and the moderate left. In this sense Brazil plays a crucial role. Brazil is a growing economy and it's a growing power, not only in the region but also in the world. Brazil is looking for a position for itself. Thus, they have made a decision to conduct an independent foreign policy. This independent foreign policy means to have a policy that is contrary to U.S. policy. We have seen this clearly when a couple of years ago Brazil along with Turkey tried to cut a nuclear deal with Iran that enabled Iran to keep its nuclear program without significant limitations.

In addition, Brazil has seen the victory of Chávez as crucial to the regional integration of the area. I don't understand the logic of such thought since regional integration is also supported by conservative governments in the region, such as the Mexican, the Colombian and the Chilean. However, the Brazilians believe that for regional integration to take place, the presence of the Bolivarian government of Venezuela is crucial. Brazil viewed the race between Capriles and Chávez last October as a competition between the right and left, even though Capriles was running on a platform that adopted the social democratic model of Brazil. So Brazil is playing a very negative role by enabling Chavismo.

So I will finalize. Bottom line, Brazil is playing a negative role in supporting Chávez, which is partly because of the currently ruling Workers' Party. The Workers' Party is very much pro-Chávez, not necessarily the president Dilma Rousseff, but the grassroots of her party tends to sympathize with the Bolivarian government.

Likewise, the Organization of American States (OAS) has failed to make the Venezuelan government accountable for its violations of democracy and human rights. Country members of the OAS have applied the terms of the democratic charter to certain governments that indeed violated human rights, but have ignored the charter when it needed to be applied to Venezuela and its allies.

I would say that is extremely important that the United States take the lead now and not just watch events. It is crucial for the U.S to make sure that the democratic charter of the OAS is respected, and in addition it should cultivate Brazil more than it is doing now. I think Brazil has a tremendous potential to be a partner of the United States because it's a growing economy, and a growing democracy, which eventually can play a similar role to the one played by the European Union. Currently Brazil is going in the direction of the third world. It is flirting with all these radical movements that are coming up in Latin America. So I think the United States should cultivate Brazil, and should take more leadership in the Organization of American States.

JON PERDUE: Thanks Nancy, for holding this very important event. I'm going to talk a bit about asymmetric warfare as practiced by Hugo Chávez prior to his passing, as well as by his allies and successors in Latin America. This type of asymmetric warfare has also become the preferred method of Mahmoud Ahmadinejad in Iran and even Bashar Assad in Syria, along with a number of their allies in the Middle East. This is often classified as a military doctrine, which it is, but about ninety percent of it is non-kinetic, or non-military, and it's that non-kinetic portion that has been developed and become fairly sophisticated over the last decade as Chávez and Fidel Castro have honed it in the region. For a little background on this type of asymmetric warfare, it was in 2004 that Hugo Chávez held what he called the first military conference on fourth generation and asymmetric warfare in Caracas, Venezuela. He brought his military together with some invited speakers, and what he did was ask his military to change their paradigm of military doctrine and their way of thinking from a conventional type of warfare to one of a "people's war," as they called it. This is where the title of my book comes from. This was originally a doctrine developed by General Giap in Vietnam that was later adopted by Fidel Castro in the 1970s. He further developed it with his brother Raul within his military and his militias in Cuba. And from there, it was adopted by Hugo Chávez.

But this also coincided at about the same time as one of Hugo Chávez's idols, Carlos the Jackal, came out as a convert to Islam while he was in jail in a French prison, and wrote a book called *Revolutionary Islam*, in which he venerated Islamic martyrs and Osama bin Laden.

But the book that Chávez utilized—I brought a copy here—to utilize as the training manual for his military, is titled *Peripheral Warfare and Revolutionary Islam*. This was written by a Spanish socialist and ideologue, and it discusses this "revolutionary" doctrine as well as things like how to build a dirty bomb, and lauds Islamic revolutionaries, because they are willing to die for the cause in the service of "The Revolution," which is, to them and their allies, an international movement.

And, though this is a non-kinetic doctrine—for instance, they have developed, to an art, things like manipulating elections both in Venezuela and in other allied countries in the region—they've also developed a very robust propaganda network that often goes unnoticed when discussing asymmetric warfare, despite its effectiveness. As far back as 1982, Fidel Castro and Muammar Qadaffi set up in Libya what's called Al-Muthaba, its Arabic name, or the Anti-Imperialism Center in English. And what this was set up to do was to coordinate and spread "revolutionary" propaganda both in the Middle East and Latin America. And, just to show examples of how this propaganda network is still in operation today, I brought some headlines that would seem to be perfectly normal in any modern Middle Eastern publication—"Israel launches Nazi-style operation against Palestinians in Gaza," "177 children in Lebanon murdered by Israeli attacks"—and the caption reads, "The indignation grows throughout the world and will not cease until an end is put to the holocaust suffered by the Lebanese and Palestinian people."

Now, that wouldn't surprise anyone as a headline in any Middle Eastern publication, but those are all up from *Granma*, the Cuban State propaganda organ. And the quote is from Ricardo Alarcon, who was one of Fidel Castro's top deputies. Recently, Iran announced HispanTV, another entrant of the recent trend of international satellite propaganda networks, which includes PressTV, Iran's English language satellite channel, Russia Today, and TeleSUR from Venezuela. When they announced HispanTV, their new Spanish-language channel, they did it in a joint press announcement with the regime in Cuba. So this was Iran utilizing the decades-old propaganda expertise of the Cuban regime to influence opinion in Latin America. It's also worth noting that in the late 1990s, Fidel Castro sent Cubans to Iran to help set up what are called "zakat committees," which are distribution networks for delving out or delivering goods, foodstuffs, and necessities for the populace within Iran, because it builds dependence, and allows the regime to better control the population. Because once you become dependent on the zakat committees, it simply becomes an old-fashioned vote-buying scheme. So Iran has been working on these types of projects with Cuba for a long time—anything that will help propagate the power of the regime, and allow them to stay in power.

I want to emphasize that this is the first time in over a decade that we've had this good an opportunity to do some good vis-à-vis Venezuela, especially when it both coincides with our policy interests and when we would be doing the right thing in the eyes of most Venezuelans—the majority of which voted against Chavismo and Hugo Chávez's chosen successor, the country's current illegitimate president. And if we do, it will not only have a positive effect in Venezuela, but once you affect Venezuela, you affect the rest of the hemisphere as well—and possibly, a lot of the proxy network that does the bidding of anti-American regimes in the Middle East.

Last week I read an article that Ambassador Roger Noriega wrote in the *Miami Herald* in which he gave a very detailed report on how the Venezuelan elections were manipulated on behalf of Chávez's hand-picked successor, Nicolás Maduro. And when I read that, it reminded me that I'd seen the name of a group before that the article mentioned had worked on rigging the elections in Venezuela. The Francisco de Miranda Front, as Roger Noriega's article mentioned as working to undermine the electoral process, was also the group that was passing out anti-American propaganda leaflets that I collected back in 2008 in Caracas, Venezuela when they were protesting outside an economic conference.

And just last month, I also picked up some more propaganda leaflets that are practically identical, in Rosario, Argentina, when I was there for another conference, five years later. What this shows is the sophistication and the widespread shepherding of everything from mundane propaganda to election-stealing that takes place under the aegis of the Cuban regime. And this has been taking place for decades, and receives far too little coverage in much of the media, especially as the mantra has become doing everything possible to normalize relations with Cuba.

And vote-rigging and propaganda is not the worst that they do. Many Venezuelans have traveled to Cuba, where they are trained in producing propaganda, in vote manipulation, and other retail political subversion. One of those who received that training was Venezuela's new president, Nicolás Maduro. But more importantly, since the 1970s—and I cover this extensively in my book, *The War of All the People*—the Cuban regime has been training people in terrorist operations as well.

Let me conclude by reiterating that, right now, we are presented with a rare opportunity in which we can affect the region in a positive way with the least amount of effort. If we are willing to only put a slight amount of pressure, and to coax our allies in the region to do the same, we can do what we have neglected to do ever since we were startled by the rabid anti-Americanism that came with the election of Hugo Chávez. It's not a lot to ask. If we would simply ask for a proper recount of the Venezuelan election, even utilizing the OAS, it would help us, the Venezuelan people, and democracy throughout the region.

Think of this. It would actually help the Maduro regime, if they actually won the election, if a recount was conducted. It would actually give Maduro legitimacy. If not, he will always be seen as an illegitimate president. But if Maduro continues in power without a proper recount, he increases the chances that he will either lose a subsequent election or will face a coup within his own ranks. And if that happens, if Maduro falls, and if PDVSA, the Venezuelan state oil company, is no longer a lifeline to Cuba, then the entire infrastructure of terrorism support, of narco-trafficking, and this international propaganda network, will also fall. This is the first chance we've had in a long time to help make that happen. And I don't think we should be shy or timid about helping our Latin American allies accomplish that.

Let me conclude by saying that I think it's great that Congressman Jeff Duncan came here to speak on this panel. He hasn't been in congress very long and he's the only one that I know of that has taken the initiative to put forward legislation asking the State Department to come up with a plan for checking Iran's subversive activities in the region. And once the Venezuelan regime falls, or is at least stunted a bit, along with the Cuban regime, a lot of the problems with Iranian influence in the region is going to get resolved by itself. But I just want to thank not only Congressman Duncan, but everyone at the Center for Security Policy that helped him with getting that legislation passed. I think it's the proper way to do it and I thank him, CSP, and I thank you all for coming.

MARTIN RODIL: Our panel has been speaking in detail very well, but now I want to take you through some facts of the problems Chávez left behind in the specific cases of Iran, Hezbollah, Latin America and other countries. People assume with Chávez's death that, well, we're in good shape. We're in good shape because Chávez is gone. But sadly, that's not the case. The situation is Chávez is dead, but the whole problem he created in fourteen years is still there and growing. And the people he left in power, now led by Maduro, are formerly the worst people in the state who respond to basically Cuba, Russia, and Iran. Regarding Iran and Hezbollah activities in the region, as much of the audience already knows and many of my colleagues have done great work analyzing and investigating, we have found very disturbing activities particularly in Venezuela that I want to walk you through. During this presentation we'll be focused only on the financial sector and terrorism support.

Well, the threat of Iran in Venezuela, as many people already know, is that over seven years a large network of entities and activities has been created that go from the military sector to many other activities. But as I said a few moments ago, the most important one has been the financial sector. Iran has found an opportunity in Venezuela's financial sector they cannot find in any other country today to get industry-wide access to war financial institutions. That previously had only been used by Iran, and we now see that infrastructure being used by Hezbollah as well as Syria. Even Syria in its current situation of imposed sanctions has been taking advantage of the infrastructure that was created. By our own personal experience, we know that the U.S. government, U.S. Treasury, as well as different law enforcement and intelligence agencies have been working on this problem for a while, but I think that there is still a lot of work to do in this regard.

I will try to go in-depth during this presentation, and quickly due to the lack of time we have. Basically this problem was created through the Iran-Venezuela alliance created after 2005 between Ahmadinejad and Hugo Chávez, and has been developed using PDVSA. This is an important key component of this relation, because PDVSA owns CITGO in the United States. Part of the financial infrastructure created by Iran and Venezuela has been taking advantage of the PDVSA financial infrastructure and the access they have in the United States financial system. The problem today as we see it is that Hugo Chávez brought a different kind of problem to a place that was already problematic, but under his regime the growth was significantly dangerous. These problems include narco-trafficking from FARC [Fuerzas Armadas Revolucionarias de Colombia] and Mexican drug cartels, Iran, the Russian mafia, Chinese mafia, Hezbollah and another Middle Eastern terrorist group that came to Venezuela and includes ETA from Spain. When you look at that, it's very difficult to understand how different entities, terrorists and criminal organizations have been able to assemble and participate on that system very effectively.

The relationship, problems, and platform described here is a heavy load, but I will try to explain how the Iranian government uses Venezuelan companies. We have detected at least 176 Iranian companies created in Venezuela over the last five years. When you look into those companies, most exist only on paper. Others exist in physical terms, but when you're trying to look into the real business of those entities, they don't. The financial activities of these companies have been very, very effective.

This financial relation started with the Banco Internacional de Desarollo, a universal bank created in Venezuela by Iran, owned by Banco Tose-e Saderat. Ambassador Noriega and myself had the opportunity recently to sit with the people at the U.S. Treasury and the OFAC [Office of Foreign Assets Control] to discuss this situation together with the district attorney's office of New York, and one of the problems we addressed was the imposed sanctions on the Banco Internacional de Desarollo. The U.S. Treasury prohibits the Banco Internacional de Desarollo to do business in dollars and to do business with U.S. entities. Well, the bank wasn't created to do that anyway. The bank was created to do business in Bolivar with Venezuelan entities that can do business with U.S. entities and can do business in dollars.

QUESTION AND ANSWER

KEN TIMMERMAN: I'm the president for the Foundation of Democracy in Iran. Martin, can you give us a little bit more detail about the involvement of U.S. banks and U.S. companies in this PDVSA network?

MARTIN RODIL: Yes. I will use an example to explain the situation more easily. During an investigation we participated in with the district attorney's office of New York two years ago, we found that there were Venezuelan bankers who were laundering money on behalf of certain groups in Venezuela who then gave [the laundered money] to the FARC, Mexican drug cartels, as well as to Hezbollah. We were trying to find out how those people were able to collocate those funds into the United States financial system, specifically the Bank of America. During the investigation we found these bankers were able to create a company who supposedly provided services and sold goods to PDVSA through a subsidiary of PDVSA in Houston, Texas, called Bariven. When we went further in the investigation we found that those transactions were supposedly for sales of drills for an oil business that supposedly came from Oklahoma but were actually never delivered. The sale never happened, but payments from PDVSA for 66 million dollars were transferred to this Houston company by the banker. Well, what we found later was the money that was coming, those 66 million dollar payments from PDVSA, was not related to any real business. It was a money laundering system created by PDVSA where they would take money in Venezuela, either for Iran or FARC, channel it through the financial system, then make the payment in the U.S. for contracts that don't exist, and then take the money to Bank of America. When Bank of America's due diligence happened they would ask,

"Where's this money coming from?" The answer is simple, that there was a contract with PDVSA, "I sold some drills to PDVSA." Well, that never happened. There are not even invoices for the delivery or anything, but the payment happened. Bank of America would stop [their investigation] there. They wouldn't inquire further because there was a payment for the account from the PDVSA subsidiary in Houston for 66 million dollars. What the banker was doing was distributing the 66 million dollars to the entities within the network. This is one of the ways they do it, but we are sure there are many, many other ways like in PDVSA bonds, for example.

KEN TIMMERMAN: So the money wasn't blocked?

MARTIN RODIL: Never was blocked. The money was distributed and paid.

FRANK GAFFNEY: Did you have a question, sir?

RUSSELL KING: Yes, I'm Russell King, and I want to direct this question to Mr. Perdue about the asymmetrical warfare and the collusion between Cuba and Venezuela. But I was wondering is there such a thing as a weather control sabotage warfare or offshore oilrig attacks, covert attacks on offshore oilrigs, or geothermal attacks that could possibly be based in Cuba? Because it seems geographically that is a perfect location as a base to do that sort of thing.

JON PERDUE: Now they've accused us, you realize, of causing storms and earthquakes to cause havoc in Venezuela before. But, look, the best thing that's happened in Cuba recently is that several oil companies have tried to drill for oil off the coast. They've all failed. But as far as that, you're getting into an area that's above my clearance level, let's say, that anybody's even capable of doing anything like that. Although we've been accused of doing it to them numerous times, I couldn't seriously address it any further than that.

FRANK GAFFNEY: Anybody else? Yes, sir.

MAN: The quick question is looking to the future. And Martin mentioned that Iran was not very heavily involved in Venezuela until 2005. And that is because Chávez and Ahmadinejad developed this very close personal relationship. I mean, so close that Ahmadinejad took Chávez to Mashhad to the tomb of the fifth Imam I believe, and came under all kinds of criticism from the clergy. So now Chávez is gone. Maduro may not be as committed as Chávez to this global vision that Chávez had. Ahmadinejad is on the way out. And his faction is out of favor with the political establishment, so who knows who's going to replace him, but it's going to be someone who's not likely to follow the same line, so what's going to happen to this relationship in view of the disappearance of two key actors, and maybe Frank may have some thoughts on this.

FRANK GAFFNEY: Well, we have a whole panel that's going to be talking about the future here in a moment, so you might want to bear with us, but Martin, you want to say a quick word on where you think this goes?

MARTIN RODIL: Yeah, well, it is true that Ahmadinejad is on his way out and his faction is out of favor with the clergy, but the presence in Venezuela is the IRGC, which is not Ahmadinejad. And those are the people in control of the network. Even if he is gone and he isn't involved, and his personal relationship that he created with Hugo Chávez is not there anymore, I think that the IRGC will do their best to sustain that network.

FRANK GAFFNEY: Let's take just one more question. I think there was another one back there. Yes, sir.

KYLE SHIDELER: This is Kyle Shideler from the Endowment for Middle East Truth. My question is along the same lines. But I wanted to ask to the extent that this narco-state exists in the infrastructure, to what extent are those individuals down for the cause? Are they profit-based? Do we have any hope of seeing in-fighting over profits and positions, or are they ideologically aligned and prepared to take this global struggle forward? I guess that's kind of my question, to any of the panel that has a thought.

JON PERDUE: In most of these throughout, from Panama when Noriega was there to Nicaragua when Ortega was there the first time, to Venezuela now, it tends to be the military that gets set up to run these things. A lot of them are just trying to maximize profit before the regime falls or before something else happens. So it's a mechanism that is almost self-perpetuating to keep the people that are there in place. The military already has the infrastructure and already has the inherent hierarchy, so there's not that much room for knocking off the head as you would in a mafia or a drug trafficking organization. But it tends to have its own self-sustaining apparatus if you set it up that way. But you get some—like Luis said, they purged eight hundred the other day, and they had all these Cubans that they put in as so-called soccer trainers within a military unit, and his job is to act as if he's training soccer players, but in reality it's to report on those that are disloyal to the Chávez regime. And they've been doing this for a decade now, so they've cleared out a lot of those that aren't loyal enough to Chavismo. So it's fairly easy to have ideologically loyal people at the top. But the structure's already there. The money is flowing in. Nobody's going to buck the system that's set up that way.

LUIS FLEISCHMAN: I want to echo what my predecessor, the other speaker said. Yes, the fact that Chávez is no longer there, that does not mean that there's not a threat. And, you know, whether it's the Iranian infrastructure or whether it's the Marco infrastructure, there are too many interests that have been created and that reminds me a little bit of the speech that was delivered by Khrushchev to the politburo after Stalin died. After that speech many people thought that there was going to be a change. Eventually, there was some change, but nothing really fundamental. So I think we should continue to watch Maduro and the Bolivarian revolution. Now, there have been some protests. And now it's going to be even worse because of what we have here, let's say in the last several weeks, is a sort of Prague Spring. The only response that these people are going to have, the regime, is not to be flexible but the opposite: radicalize the revolution. And Maduro actually referred to the fact, we are going to radicalize the revolution. And he spoke about revolution within a revolution, which is like a page taken from Cuba fifty-something years ago. In addition, the idea that the reduction of the oil price is going to bring about the collapse of the regime is a myth. A poor regime can still survive. Think about Cuba. There is no need for oil to sustain a regime like that. It is based on pure repression.

We need to continue to promote democracy to put a stop to the expansion of the Bolivarian revolution by at least making sure that the OAS democratic charter is properly applied. This doesn't mean that we'll solve all the problems. But at this point we are not doing anything, so we need to start with something.

FRANK GAFFNEY: Well, we're going to be thinking and talking about it considerably more momentarily. Thank you very much.

PANEL TWO:

DOUGLAS FARAH, SENIOR FELLOW AT THE INTERNATIONAL ASSESSMENT AND STRATEGY CENTER, PRESIDENT OF IBI CONSULTANTS AND FORMER INVESTIGATIVE REPORTER AND FOREIGN CORRESPONDENT FOR THE *WASHINGTON POST*

> Topic: Drug trafficking and the Bolivarian revolutions of Ecuador, Bolivia and Argentina

MICHAEL BRAUN, FORMER ASSISTANT ADMINISTRATOR AND CHIEF OF OPERATIONS, U.S. DRUG ENFORCEMENT ADMINISTRATION.

> Topic: Hezbollah: Iran's Most Important Proxy and Venezuela's Most Important Criminal Partner

ROGER NORIEGA, FORMER ASSISTANT SECRETARY OF STATE FOR THE WESTERN HEMISPHERE AND PRESIDENT OF VISION AMERICAS

> Topic: The Impact of the Venezuelan Narcoterrorist State on Latin America and U.S. National Security

MODERATOR: FRANK J. GAFFNEY, JR., PRESIDENT AND CEO, THE CENTER FOR SECURITY POLICY

DOUGLAS FARAH: I think listening to the last panel, the question is what happens now without Chávez. And I think a large part of the answer, what happens now is Argentina. I think if you look at Argentina, which historically, I've just been spending a lot of time there and I just did a long report on Argentina and all of these issues. I'll be happy to give it to you online, it's available in both English and Spanish. If you look at the role Argentina has played in the last multiple years in drug trafficking, it's grown exponentially just because the government doesn't really care. That you've had the Kirchners, Néstor followed by his wife Cristina. And if you look—one of the things I've started looking at, at the request of a particular client, was the precursor chemical flows through Argentina, which is fascinating because suddenly Argentina was awash in cocaine and it has actually the highest per capita cocaine use in the world today. Brazil is the second highest user population after the United States

27

in the world today. So you see the impact of the drug trade largely driven by the fact that Peru and Bolivia are now producing HTL, the white powder you stick up your nose, which they had not been doing for many years when the communes were in control. Now it's flooding the markets and a lot of it's going to West Africa and Europe, and others have done a lot of work on that.

But when you saw the precursor in Argentina, was ephedrine, which was used for methamphetamines. And if you looked at it in 2008, the legal requirement for the Argentine pharmaceutical industry was less than one ton and they were importing twenty-eight tons. So one might think there's something a little bit off on the economic rationale of that. And it turns out they're shipping loads of that then up to Mexico. There were no import controls at all. So it wasn't actually illegal. There were several big massacres down there. The Mexican cartels have moved in. It got really ugly. And they suddenly said, okay, we're going to cut this down. They put in some new export-import controls and it dropped a little bit and now it's back up to above twenty tons again this year. So you see the complete sort of absence of interest in controlling the precursor flows and the cocaine flows. But I think what was most interesting and I think that if the conversation is focused largely on Venezuela today, and I think in that context Venezuela has certainly been important, but you can't ignore the financial structure and drug flow structure and the Bolivarian structure in general, the roles that both Ecuador and Argentina play in the finances end of drug trafficking.

So that's what I'm going to focus a little bit on. If you look at how Argentina has evolved in the last just really year, maybe less than a year, President Kirchner has decided that her fate lies with the Bolivarian revolution and not elsewhere, as she's pursued a series of really dramatically irrational economic policies. Not driven so much by a coherent ideology as by a vision of herself as second to Evita Peron. And I just finished a paper which should be published this weekend, I hope, that looks at the groups surrounding her. And there's a really interesting group that's called La Cámpora. They're a group of young people, mostly under forty years old, brought together by Cristina's son, Máximo, who have this really—cause I've read a lot of writings they publish a lot—really strange utopian vision that's a mixture of Marxism, fascism, Peronism, and all of these different things that is driving the current economic policy in Argentina. So if you want to understand why they've run off the rails so dramatically, look to this group of people who are completely, you know, essentially live on a different planet. They don't believe that the laws of economics apply to

Argentina and they're making their best cases to prove it doesn't as the economy goes down the toilet. In that group of people, a lot of them come out of the Montonero movement, the guerilla movement in the 1970s and 80s. Several of them are children of those who disappeared from the military dictatorship, so they have a definite sort of trajectory in their own personal lives. And what they've decided—and this is driving I think their alliance with Iran that you see emerging in Argentina—they've decided that the United States is no longer welcome. They have this Falklands and this issue with Great Britain and a whole series of issues, so they want to make Argentina part of the Bolivarian alliance and they've moved very dramatically as they do that to this very strange and inexplicable, at this point, alliance with Iran. You know as well as I do, 1994, the AMIA bombing, the biggest terrorist attack by Islamic radicals in the hemisphere before 9/11. And Argentina maintained a consistent policy of distance with Iran. They walked out of the United Nations when the Iranian president spoke and all these things. They suddenly negotiated, which became public in January of this year, this secret memorandum of understanding between Iran and Argentina.

And the crux of that understanding is that they're going to throw out the legal investigations that led to the Interpol red notices against seven Iranian officials including the current defense minister Ahmed Vahidi, and in exchange, they're going to do a joint investigation essentially designed to prove that Iran is not involved, although there's overwhelming evidence that it was a joint Iran/Hezbollah operation that carried out those attacks. What does Iran get out of this? It's quite easy to see that the thing that hurts them most in the international community still is that seven of their top leaders are wanted by Interpol. They theoretically can't travel. They do travel. Ahmed Vahidi went to Bolivia in 2011 to inaugurate the joint military academy. One of the things that John was talking about, the asymmetrical warfare that happened at the academy that they have in Santa Cruz, Bolivia designed to teach this book as military doctrine to the pan-American military officer corps that goes down in their training. And Vahidi, knowing that he was wanted by Interpol, knowing that he would not be arrested in Bolivia actually went to the inauguration of that school, and why is precisely because the Iranians are putting in several million dollars into that infrastructure and beginning to teach their own military doctrine. The stated goal, if you looked on their website of the school is to eradicate any last vestiges of U.S. military doctrine in Latin America. So it's pretty clear. They're not very subtle about how they manifest what they want to do. But this dynamic with Iran and Venezuela, and Argentina and Iran, is part of I think the new triangulation effect. I think that if the Iranians had been aware that there are going to be significant problems as the Venezuelan system falls apart, they need another country. Bolivia doesn't provide the infrastructure they necessarily need. Ecuador doesn't have the bandwidth to do all they need to do. And so they've pushed heavily into Argentina, which does. And if you look at how Argentine trade with Iran has grown, it's grown by several hundred percent in the last several years.

Well over a billion dollars now in bilateral trade, most of it is legal, and it is a huge surplus for Argentina. They export beef and wheat and all kinds of stuff to Iran, which Iran really needs it. The question is, what does Iran get out of the relationship? What does Argentina get out of this new relationship? It's clear, like I said, what Iran gets. They will get ultimately some sort of legitimacy in their leadership by having Ahmed Vahidi having his charges dropped. The memorandum of understanding, when it was finally published, is an incredibly opaque and stupid document. It's completely incoherent. And anytime there's been a divergence of opinion, the Argentinians said initially all of the Iranian officials, according to the memorandum, were saying would be questioned by Argentine prosecutors. And Iran said, no, they're not. Okay, sorry. And they said, well, okay, certain other things in Iran, Iran said, no, that's not right and Argentina said, okay. And Argentina said, none of the Interpol notices will be dropped. And Iran said a few weeks ago, yes, they will be dropped. Then you can be pretty sure that Iran's going to win that debate. So I think that if you look at the expansion efforts into a real economy with real banks doing interesting things, Argentina is the place to focus.

And I just want to close by talking a little bit about Ecuador, because what makes Ecuador so attractive is that it is a dollarized economy. And I think we often overlook the value of that dollarized economy in the ability of Iran to move money through the international system. And one of the things that passed almost unnoticed, although there was some public reporting on it, was that in January of 2012, President Correa of Ecuador met with Ahmadinejad on a state visit and we acquired the minutes of that meeting, which then Correa acknowledged were authentic. President Correa essentially offers the Iranians an Ecuadorian bank to launder their money: COFIEC Bank. Ahmadinejad said we need help with breaking sanctions. Correa said, well, I have this little bank, some state receivership here, why don't you use that bank? And then he appoints the president of the Central Bank of Ecuador to go to Iran to negotiate use of Koviet Bank for Iranian sanction busting purposes. And what was really interesting is that they did their first—and I've read their paper on this, if you want to see it, it's all public sources out there and documented—but the first thing that the delegation of Ecuador did was go to Russia.

Why did they go to Russia? Because Russia is the only country where Iranian banks don't have—or only one of the few where they can still have correspondent relationships. So they go to Russia, set up correspondent relationships between COFIEC Bank and the same bank where the Iranian banks are. Then they go to Iran to negotiate the sale of COFIEC Bank or the use of COFIEC Bank. And the minutes describe the meetings with four different sanctioned Iranian banks. They're fully aware that the Iranian banks are under both UN and U.S. and EU sanctions, all three. And one of the banks says, well, this is great. We would like to use COFIEC Bank, and how about if we have an encrypted system of communications so that we can talk back and forth with each other without the outside world knowing. We'll have an encrypted telex and we'll keep the deciphering code in the Iranian Embassy in Ecuador. Now, that's not a normal banking relationship. It's not how you normally open correspondence, relations, unless you want something to hide. So I think the focus on the future of the revolution is going to be—of the Iran relationship and the Bolivarian revolution—is going to be a great deal outside of Venezuela's role. I think they're well aware of the chaos that's going to be coming into Venezuela as either Maduro radicalizes, weakens, he won't be able to keep the factions together, all of those things. And they've already moved a considerable amount of their economic infrastructure to Ecuador. Not the bulk of it, but it's been shifting out. Correa has made it known in meetings in Cuba, when they've all been together there, he views himself as the Bolivarian successor to Chávez. He wants to become – he knows he was smarter than Chávez. He knows that Evo Morales can't do it, he knows Maduro is going to be weak. And he views himself as a natural successor. So I think Ecuador's role will grow substantially and I think Argentina is the sort of new element that will keep the process alive in ways that work. We otherwise would not have predicted, had it been a closed system, how it would end. I'll leave it there.

MICHAEL BRAUN: Good afternoon. Well, good morning, still. Nancy and Frank, thank you very much for the invitation to participate and to speak, and to address the very distinguished group of folks who are gathered here today. I'd like to thank you, as well as the members of your team Frank, you know, Ben and Anita and others, for doing all that you do to keep us safe here at home. And I mean that with all sincerity because groups like yours keep the hot topics at the forefront and that's what we absolutely have to do and we have to do more of. Some have mentioned

Congressman Jeff Duncan and the outstanding job that he's done in a pretty short time. But I cannot think of another member of congress, quite frankly, that has pushed the topic to the forefront that I'm going to focus on, and that's Hezbollah, their growing involvement in the global drug trade. And what all that means to us here at home and the threat that that poses to us at home.

I always try to come up with a title of a presentation that will accurately capture my comments. And mine is, Hezbollah: Iran's Most Important Proxy; Venezuela's Most Important Terrorist and Criminal Partner. And thanks to the previous panel members. They added a couple other aspects or dimensions to that that are critically important. They added the importance of the revolutionary armed forces of Colombia—the FARC. And obviously, there's been a lot of talk of Iran. We have to look at all four of these [threats], not as singular, distinct, individual, disparate threats. We have to look at them collectively—as interconnected threats. Individually, I don't think any of them pose a really, a tremendous threat to us at this point in time. But collectively, they really are an awesome, an extraordinary threat. Most of my comments are going to be from the thirty thousand foot level and I'll come down to the treetops occasionally just to drive a few points home. But it's important to understand a couple of things right up front.

Of the fifty terrorist organizations that our country has identified and formally designated as foreign terrorist organizations, groups that pose a threat to our nation and our way of life, as well as other freedom loving nations around the world, well over fifty—well over half of those fifty are now involved in one or more aspects of the global drug trade. And that's a topic that I could talk about all day long. But that poses some very, very unique and related kinds of threats that I think you will be able to parse out of what I'm saying as I move through this. It's important also to understand that I'm not just talking about the Western Hemisphere's usual suspects. I'm not just talking about the FARC, Sindero Luminoso and some of the others that have come and gone over the past many decades. But I'm also talking about groups like Hezbollah, more and more al-Qaeda, the Taliban and others, that are involved now in one or more aspects of the global drug trade.

I can't remember which one of the panelists initially said it is money that keeps these groups alive, but they are absolutely correct. They have to keep their movements alive. And quite frankly, we've done yeoman's work at prosecuting our global war on terror. We know, state sponsorship for terrorism is on the decline. If you don't subscribe to that, I think you would agree that we've forced it much deeper underground, which increases the cost a great deal more to do business and to support a terrorist group. And we've also done yeoman's work in identifying very powerful, private funding streams that pump money into the war chests of terrorist organizations that are hell bent on destroying our way of life. We have significantly disrupted those funding streams as well. So more and more of these groups have to turn to the global drug trade, and to other types of transnational criminal activity to fund their operations.

But let's talk about Hezbollah for just a minute. Just ten short years ago, the Hezbollah was not heavily involved in the global cocaine trade. They were moving small amounts of cocaine, you know, ten to fifteen kilogram quantities from out of the tri-border area, albeit on a daily basis, certainly weekly basis, into other parts of the world where they could sell it and make enormous profits. But if you flash forward to today, they're moving multi-ton quantities now into – or out of the Andean region into Venezuela, across the Atlantic, into West Africa, into North Africa, onward to Europe, where the skyrocketing demand for cocaine and some other emerging markets in that part of the world have absolutely resulted in Hezbollah's meteoric rise in the global cocaine trade. That activity has introduced them to new, extremely important strategic partners like the FARC, the Mexican drug trafficking cartels and indigenous organized crime in the western part of Africa, to terrorist organizations like al-Qaeda in the Islamic Maghreb and others. And again, this just adds to this very, very nasty milieu.

I describe this really as the potpourri of global organized crime. But it is very much all coming together. One country, more than any other, facilitates and enables this activity, and that country is Venezuela. It has become the, really the axis, the point of departure for the vast majority of cocaine that is now headed up the old Caribbean route and across the Atlantic into Europe, where the Hezbollah is reaping not tens of millions of dollars a year, folks, in profits, but hundreds of millions of dollars a year in profit. I'll go into more detail on that in just a minute. So what's the confluence of Hezbollah, Iran, the FARC, and Venezuela? Well, what does it mean for the safety and security of our country and other places around the world? I'll get into that more in just a minute, but I think most of you would say, well, we're not really sure. No one is really sure what it means. But I can tell you what I do know. I am a practitioner, folks. After thirty-five years in this business, it ain't good. It's not good. And we'll drill into that with a couple of other comments here. Ahmadinejad, I don't think anybody's really mentioned this, hopefully most of you know it, and Iran,

Ahmadinejad and Iran have opened six additional embassies in Latin America in just the past five or six years. They now have eleven embassies in Latin America: in the countries of Argentina, Bolivia, Brazil, Chile, Colombia, Cuba, Ecuador, Mexico, Nicaragua, Uruguay and Venezuela. And I believe in the not too distant, well, I'm sorry, they have also established one in Ecuador. Not surprising to this growth, we're seeing an exponential growth in the presence of the Quds force. The special forces arm of the IRGC that is responsible for clandestine operations abroad, including assassinations.

We'll touch more on that in just a minute. This illicit threat—and that's what it is—it's an illicit threat, has been, thanks to criminality, thanks to terrorism, it's been evolving for many, many years. It didn't just start yesterday. And like any other asymmetric threat, once the fire starts, and we allow the flames to grow, and they're spread by the wind, it becomes a threat that almost cannot be extinguished. It's almost impossible to totally extinguish it. And I'd like to also say, and add to what some others have said, because I honestly believe that because Hugo Chávez is no longer with us, not much is going to change with respect to Venezuela. And the reason I say that is because the fourteen years worth of filth and nastiness that are contained in the regime have been institutionalized within the political and the security infrastructure of that country. And the politicians, at the very highest levels, and security leaders at the very highest levels are now getting even fatter and ever more filthy rich by the day. I go back to, it's all about the money. There's way too much at stake for them now to give it up. I've just been told the hook's coming out, so let me wrap this up as quickly as I can. This isn't just Mike Braun talking, not a former senior guy from DEA. Robert Mueller, the head of the FBI, Mike Chertoff, when he was the Secretary of the Department of Homeland Security, both testified before congress that we need to stay focused on al-Qaeda. Al-Qaeda is a real threat, but the real threat is Hezbollah. They [Hezbollah] have an organizational and an operational sophistication, or level of sophistication, that al-Qaeda could only hope to have. They have established a global footprint.

Now let me sum it up like this. As tensions continue to heat up between our country and Iran, Iran and Israel, we have to be thinking about some things. If, I suppose I should say when, based on what we're reading in the papers, the final development of bunker busting bombs that can finally hit Iran's nuclear production capacity—when we hit them, what is Iran's response going to be? How are they going to strike back at us? The answer—there is really only one answer—they will strike back at us through Hezbollah and the Quds force. Congressman King, his comments not mine, held a hearing that I testified before—his Committee on Homeland Security back in March of last year, his comments, he's been briefed by high level government officials, that there are at least two hundred Hezbollah operatives that are operating on American soil today. Listen, folks, you know, it's not if they can hit us, it's when they can hit us. And what kind of damage they can do. I can promise you this, that they have got the ability to make what we witnessed, the bad as well as the good, in Boston just a few short weeks ago, look like child's play. And I don't want to diminish what happened. But they have got the ability to make that look like child's play. We can't let this happen. Thanks.

ROGER NORIEGA: You know, I had to put myself in the position of the State Department thinking about president Obama's visit to Mexico and Central America, because he went to Mexico at a time when President Enrique Peña Nieto is declaring fairly brazenly in the U.S. media that he's going to change their approach to fighting the drug problem in their country, to quell violence on the street with a different strategy. A lot of us remember the truces that his party made at various levels with the narco-traffickers. And that is something that is just completely unacceptable in this new era where we hold governments more accountable than ever in terms of their complicity with narco-trafficking and narco-terrorist organizations.

So the president says let's pivot to bilateral cooperation regarding economic cooperation. For President Obama, it's impossible to do that. And it suggests to me the chilling reality that he doesn't understand what we're confronting in this hemisphere, which is a narco-terrorist phenomenon that has metastasized in this hemisphere and fuelling bloody conflicts in Central America and Mexico, and drug consumption and crime in the United States. The so-called drug war can be traced back many decades. Most have failed to recognize the dangerous new role being played by a narco-state in Venezuela today. Venezuela government officials have close operational ties with Colombian narco-traffickers and guerrillas, Mexican cocaine kingpins, Central American operatives, politicians, and Hezbollah terrorists that form a criminal network that sows lawlessness, bloodshed and mayhem in many of these countries—including the United States. Moreover, Venezuela's foreign policy has made alliances with individuals in these countries, who abuse the electoral process, to take office and decimate the rule of law and democratic institutions and also end their cooperation with us in fighting the narco threat. This happened in Honduras. All of the fuss that Chávez was interested in 2009 about keeping Manuel

Zelaya in power was about keeping a link in the drug chain in place. And now Zelaya's wife is running for president of Honduras and backed by these same narco-terrorist elements. The same may be happening in El Salvador and in a grand scale right on our border with Mexico. Some may assess this cooperation between the narcos and terrorists as a mere marriage of convenience between different criminal elements. Or just the modus operandi of international drug syndicates finding another way of doing business. Instead, I think that this criminal activity is part of a conscious strategy of these countries, led by Venezuela, to wage asymmetrical warfare against U.S. interests, allies and our security as well.

It also works to undermine the democratic institutions and overwhelm law enforcement in order to accommodate criminal activity. Making matters worse is that Venezuela's de facto government is wrestling with a crisis of illegitimacy and insolvency. Its complicity with lucrative criminal organizations and criminal enterprises will only grow. This criminal-political threat requires a much more robust analysis and coordinated response from exposing Venezuela's support for Colombian and Islamic terrorist groups; identifying narco-terrorist activities in Central America and Mexico; imposing sanctions against entities, including state-run entities that are being used to aid and abet criminal transactions; dismantling transnational money laundering schemes; exposing politicians who work in the service of criminals; and bolstering the capability of responsible democratic governments to confront this threat.

Unless the U.S. government begins to understand, to speak clearly and to take seriously the threat emanating from Venezuela's criminal regime, it cannot mobilize an effective response among our partners. And until the United States does that, governments will continue to tolerate lawlessness on the part of Venezuela. They could make truces with criminals in order to quell violence in their territory, and will grow ever more vulnerable to the narco-terrorist threat that aims to attack us in our neighborhood. My colleague, Martin Rodil, referred to the leadership of the Venezuelan government, their involvement, and their complicity in narco-trafficking from the current head of the national assembly, Diosdado Cabello, who is the capo di tutti capi, according to Eladio Aponte Aponte, and the Supreme Court justice who defected to the United States about a year ago. He named sixty military officers that are involved in narco-trafficking. Senior Chavista officials engage routinely in lucrative schemes involving Hezbollah front companies, Colombian terrorist groups, narco-traffickers, Venezuelan financial institutions, and even in PDVSA. Which I say is an oil company that really operates as a drug trafficking organization that produces some oil on the side. Their production is down forty percent since Chávez took office, but they seem to have the same amount of money as they always had. This is extraordinarily dangerous.

These politicians, active duty and retired military officers transport tons of cocaine into Central America, Mexico, the Caribbean, the United States, West Africa and Europe as Mr. Braun has explained. In private, one senior official in the State Department refers to this as an "explosion of cocaine from Venezuela." Very conservative estimates in their reports say that it's at least doubled. But I think it's much, much greater than that. Every day ten or twelve or fifteen planes leave on their way to Honduras. Every day. And airborne traffic only represents twenty percent of all the cocaine going into Honduras, so there are extraordinary amounts of money involved, generated for their political activities. And Zelaya, the former president whose restoration to power was advocated by the United States, even though they knew at the time that he was involved in narco-trafficking. I told them about this because I heard it internally from their sources. They had three people leave our embassy in Honduras in the years prior to Zelaya's oust because they could not stomach the fact that our embassy was turning a blind eye to drug trafficking by Zelaya; and that's the guy that we advocated in our foreign policy to restore to power after he was ousted.

It is a little known fact that the world's most powerful cocaine smuggler and head of the Sinaloa Cartel, Joaquin Chapo Guzman, spent the better part of the year 2010 in Venezuela, running his operations from outside Caracas and later Margarita Island. And now we have information that he left the country over a year ago. But we knew and U.S. officials knew at the time that he was there.

How does Hezbollah figure into this? In the Americas, Hezbollah relies on complicity with the Venezuelan state and partnerships with oil financed Mexican and Colombian narco-traffickers and guerilla groups that have in place the sophisticated smuggling and money laundering activities in the region. They've tapped into that preexisting network. That's how they managed to move so far and so fast in about five years. They use these ties as a way of raising money, laundering funds, sharing tactics, training sleeper cells and reaching out and touching U.S. territory, as Martin has alluded. This plot to blow up a restaurant in the heart of our nation's capital, everybody talks of the plot on the Saudi ambassador. Quite frankly, I don't care about the Saudi ambassador. They were going to blow up a restaurant in Washington, D.C. That was detected by DEA folks, and they got that information. Why? Because Hezbollah had reached out to somebody they thought was a Mexican narco-trafficker to carry out the bombing.

The DEA folks went from office to office and were laughed out of the offices because there are so many people who can't think outside the box and would think that Hezbollah would not have the audacity to do this. Until they got a wire transfer from an IRGC operative who they know killed dozens of Americans in bombings, they started to take it seriously. So thank God these people are capable of thinking outside the box. I'll refer you to—it's on the web, to a network, money laundering network, run by a man, Iman Juna, that U.S. law enforcement detected that he has frozen assets of his various operatives. That was an international network that linked Mexican, Colombian drug smugglers using entities in various countries including Venezuela and others to launder hundreds of millions of dollars a month until it was detected. This is a profound threat. President Obama told a Miami journalist in July, 2012, "my sense is that what Mr. Chávez has done over the last several years has not had a serious national security impact on the United States." This shows a really startling failure to comprehend the grave and growing threat that they pose. Not only to our security, but to the security and the political stability of the Western Hemisphere as a whole. So I do pay tribute to the fact that Congress is paying a lot of attention and especially to Congressman Duncan and to Chairman Mike McCall and I hope Congressman Salmon will take this up as the chairman of the subcommittee. Let me just wrap this up very quickly. Recommendations. We shouldn't, knowing all we know about these things, legitimize the Maduro regime, which stole an election on April 14th. The president has managed not to say those things, but you saw a statement yesterday from assistant secretary of state for Western Hemisphere affairs, Roberta Jacobson, referring to, quote, the forty-nine percent of people who voted for Capriles. She has no idea that forty-nine percent voted for Capriles. There's never been a recount. The president of the United States doesn't even recognize the results.

And that is a signal to Maduro that, don't worry, the career diplomats are going to sort this out for you, and they're going to normalize relationships with a narco-state. That has to, at the very least, be on the table, you know, the drug trafficking involvement. We're already hearing signals that they're ready to give up some narco generals. You know, and just name a name and we'll throw one over the fence to you. Well, you know, Diosdado Cabello for starters, the president of the national assembly, would be great. But it reminds me of the guy that writes to the IRS and says, I cheated on my taxes five years ago and I haven't been able to sleep since, here's a hundred thousand dollars. If I still can't sleep, I'll send you the rest. So this is, you know, a real threat. And I do understand that the DEA and OFAC and others, that have worked assiduously on this. But where are the indictments from Eric Holder's justice department? We know there are some sealed indictments. Why aren't they unsealed? And there are various reasons.

But there should be indictments against these principals of the Venezuelan government. There should be sanctions, at the very least, against PDVSA or these various entities, or operatives of PDVSA. Who carry out these parallel commercial businesses? And we have the names and we've given the names to OFAC, along with correspondence that points out this criminal activity. So we need to press for those indictments. We need more intelligence capability in this hemisphere. General Kelly, who's the new commander of Southcom said very clearly in his posturing statement, "we do not have the resources to address this problem." And he spoke more specifically about this threat than his two previous predecessors have in the past. We need to cooperate with our allies in Latin America, Canada and Europe and have a good dialogue with intelligence and law enforcement and armed forces organizations so they understand this threat. So to conclude, this narco-terrorism on our doorstep, perpetrated by Mexican and South American narco-traffickers, Colombian terrorist guerillas and Hezbollah with Iranian and Venezuelan complicity demands a response from those whose job it is to keep us safe. Our government has to take these measures unilaterally and/or with willing partners to disrupt and dismantle these illicit operations and neutralize these unacceptable threats. That's the very least that we can expect of our government. Thank you very much.

QUESTION AND ANSWER

MAN: About the case about the hiring of the Mexican DTO [drug trafficking organization] do the bombing in Washington, D.C., there's plenty of Hezbollah running around the U.S. I mean, we know that from other investigations. You know, why not use one of them? Why use the Mexicans? Is it plausible deniability, and if you use plausible deniability, then where's the terror? I mean, isn't the fun of terrorism about strategic communications of fear me, fear me lots, and then if you have plausible deniability, you kind of lose that. The other question was for Roger. I have a theory that there're different factions—I'm Venezuelan by the way, born in America—and I have a question about, I think there are different factions in the Venezuelan government, some are more ideological and view the drugs thing as a great way to fund that. And some people are just having lots of fun making lots of money. Hezbollah's thrilled because they're just, you know, it's sort of plane loads of drugs—big plane loads rather than little ones. So given that you have different factions with slightly different motivations, how will that fracture as the PSUV [Venezuela's ruling party] fractures?

MICHAEL BRAUN: Well, first of all, great question or questions. With respect to, you know, why not claim credit yourselves and use Hezbollah operatives. I mean, it has everything to do with deniability, and understand that Hezbollah are masters at just that. You know, and why? I mean, they don't want to commit suicide, for God's sake, you know, in the act. They know and can certainly understand what our response would be. So if you can blame it on a, you know, a member of the ultra-violent Los Zetas, or someone else, then by all means, do it. Carry it out. Let someone else take credit for it, or blame it on someone else, protect yourself as best you can. But, you know, that example, I think more than anything else, speaks to the importance of Hezbollah and the Quds force. The Quds force was right in the middle of that as well. It's important to understand something else. Where you find Hezbollah, you will always find the Quds force. They [Quds Force] built it [Hezbollah], they developed it. They built it, they continue to manage and direct much of their activities globally.

But it is, you know, that example—I can't think of a better example than that one that speaks to what Hezbollah really is. Hezbollah is Iran's fleet of aircraft carriers. They are the weapons delivery system for Iran. Iran's got the ability to strike us at home and any of our interests anywhere in the world through its fleet of aircraft carriers, the Hezbollah—managed and directed by the Quds force.

ROGER NORIEGA: I think you can identify these factions that you alluded to with that rivalry within the ruling party, between Diosdado Cabello and Maduro. Cabello is a military guy and is thought to have the confidence of people in the military who think like him. He's sat on all the promotion boards for most of these general officers and others. He's not considered ideological and he's actually hostile to Cuba. But he's up to his eyeballs in narco-trafficking. Maduro, on the other hand, is an ideologue and is puppet of the Cubans; and he's doing their bidding. Maduro is much more likely to continue the money going to Cuba, for example. That's why the Cubans insisted that he take power. Cabello, on the other hand, I have heard rumors that he's said he'll shove the Cubans out. "I'll push the Cubans out if we can make some kind of arrangement." And what went through my head was, well, don't ask; you're not doing us any favors, shoving the Cubans out. Shove the Iranians and Hezbollah out and then we'll talk. So he would do that and there are going to be people who are going to want to cash in their chips and go live in their villas that they've built in Milan and Madrid and other places. And they don't want to give that money to Bolivia and Nicaragua, because they will be spending their inheritance, right? So there will be that natural tension between those who want to continue this sort of ideological foreign policy, which is altogether provocative and those who say, look, this is not personal, it's business, and let's do business. And that's going to really break them apart. There's a lot of sort of negative energy within that ruling party. And that's just—that's without dealing with a disintegrating economy and a criminal situation that's absolutely out of control and all of the other things that Chavismo has wrought in that country.

ERIN ANDERSON: I'm Erin Anderson and I monitor the activity between Mexico and the U.S. border. So your comments were extraordinarily relevant, we're seeing it up close and personal. And I'm also monitoring the comprehensive immigration bill that's been, you know, in the senate. I'm alarmed that neither of you were able to testify in the senate on this bill, and I'd like to ask for both of your comments on how the senate immigration comprehensive bill, what will be the ramifications given what you've seen and observed and talked about and this amnesty bill?

MICHAEL BRAUN: Well, I mean listen, my comment is this. Really, I don't care how tough we crack down on immigration, and I think the ambassador would agree with me. He's seen the same thing in many other border locations. I don't care how hard you crack down, no matter what legislation you come up with, highly sophisticated organizations like Mexican drug trafficking organizations—and, by the way, folks, they didn't just get their start ten or twelve years ago, they've been in the business for the better part of seven decades. They will, listen, they will find their way around, under, over or through any blockade that you put up. They are the most cagey, intuitive group of individuals that you will ever find. What I will also say to that is, and that's why groups like Hezbollah and Quds force find them critically important and they're doing everything that they possibly can to build rock solid, enduring relations with these groups, because they understand the strategic importance of that border and the fact that the Mexican cartels now dominate drug trafficking in over five hundred cities throughout the United States. That's extremely important to them [Hezbollah]—their [Mexican cartels'] ratlines, their cachet sites, and their safe houses. They're already in place. And they can exploit it and leverage it for all that it's worth simply through developing solid, enduring relations and there is no criminal or terrorist group in the world that I know of that is better at that than Hezbollah.

ROGER NORIEGA: I authored a piece that was published in one of these Hill newspapers, saying that comprehensive immigration reform should include a foreign policy component which is about helping, not with tons of aid, but helping generate private sector activity in these countries and creating jobs. There should be a conscious effort at doing that. We also want to include our security assistance to these countries. We have to do more. We talk about Mexico's drug war, but it's not Mexico's drug war. It's our drug war and Mexico is fighting it. They were until last week. And that's going to become a problem for us. So I think we need to do more on that security—that foreign policy part of this immigration issue.

I believe we have to deal with the immigrant population here, folks that are here illegally, in some responsible way. And it's going to be a very complicated legislative process, and I hope that we can produce something meaningful. I come at this, as you might imagine, from a national security perspective. Including, therefore, securing the border as much as we possibly can to honest commerce and honest crossings and we can't do that with an immigration system that is not functioning. We should have an immigration system that accommodates our labor force requirements, whatever they may be. People come here and contribute to our economy because we are a nation of immigrants who have always contributed to our economy. Immigrants start and create jobs and all of those sorts of economic activities. So I think from a lot of different standpoints, we need to have some kind of comprehensive bill. But that's what a lot of folks who are skeptics are insisting upon, is border security, and I am a hundred percent on board with that, too.

www.ingramcontent.com/pod-product-compliance
Lightning Source LLC
Chambersburg PA
CBHW021339290326
41933CB00038B/980